These people help me catch and kick.

These people help me if I'm sick.

These people help me read and learn.

These people help my wheels to turn.

These people help me with my teeth.

These people help those in grief.

These people keep us safe from harm.

These people help if you break your arm.

These people help out with a hose.

My mum helps me to blow my nose.

These people help your mind feel well.

A nurse once helped me when I fell.

My dad helps tuck me into bed.

To help me sleep, I have my ted.

Many people help I guess.

But no one will help me clean my mess.

Activities

Can you name the person and how they help you?

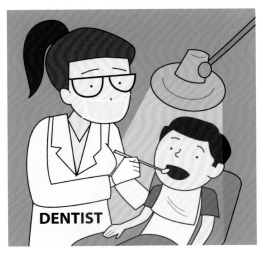

Can you name the people and how they help you?

Can you name the people and how they help you?

Can you name the person and how they help you?